FITNESS IS FUN
OUTDOOR Vol 2, Ed 1

LINDA J. KEEP, Ph.D.

Copyright © 2019 Linda J. Keep, Ph.D.

All rights reserved. No part of this book may be reproduced or transmitted, in any form or by any means, either in whole or in part, included but not limited to information storage and retrieval systems, electronic, mechanical, photocopy, recording, etc. without written permission from the copyright holders. Exceptions are brief passages for reviews.

ISBN: 978-0-9952922-9-1 (Paperback)

Book design by Linda J. Keep, Ph.D.
Images provided by Adobe Stock

Printed in the United States of America

First edition, First printing 2019.

Published By: Psychology Center Inc.
Sherwood Park, AB, Canada

www.psychologypublications.com

A GIFT FOR YOU!

Visit *www.psychologypublications.com/Books* to download
12 free maze puzzles & 13 fun coloring pages.

THIS BOOK

BELONGS TO

_____

Can you find me? I am "peek-a-boo."

A dragon's meadow
Offers play
For every dragon
Every day.

Yet today
The meadow sits empty,
Where are our friends?
There used to be plenty!

Stephen says,

"They stay indoors.
They eat and eat
And grow too big
For their feet."

"Come play,"
 We say.
"Come outdoors."
"Yeah! Okay!"

"I make a plan
To meet my friends.
It is time to play.
Indoors ends."

"I like to splash."
"Wet and fresh,"
Monique says,
"Water play is the best."

"Oh!" Shouts Bee.
"A reflection of me!
It is ME
times THREE!"

"That's okay!
Large or stout,
Tall or small,
Play is what it's all about."

"I like sand,
 Swings,
  Monkey bars,
  But slides
   are king!"

"Whee!" Says Landon.
 He slides to the bottom.
 Then climbs again,
  His first ride forgotten.

"Golf anyone?"
Rowan calls out.
Friends stand in line.
"Yes!" They shout.

Fitness is fun!
Fitness is play!
Not hard work.
I can play all day!

Wheels on a board,
Or on your feet,
I think skating
Is really neat.

Twist and turn,
Tumble and fall.
Bend and laugh,
One and all.

Soccer! Paul scores.
He scores and scores.
He scores galore!
Like never before.

"Jog, Michelle!"
"Run."
"Jump!"
"Home run!"

"The clickity-clackity
Of my feet.
On the bark and rocks
Make a musical beat."

Hide and seek!
That's what we'll play.
Take a peek.
"No way! No way!"

Lenna says,
"We'll hide all day!
Till the sun
Goes away."

Tag!
You tag me!
I tag you.
Yippee! Yippee!

"King of the castle!"
 Shouts Evie.
"Win the flag!
 And king I'll be!"

"Treats are okay
Once in a while.
Big chocolate ones
Make me smile."

Rollie's breath
Melts cones quickly
And makes his feet
A little sticky.

"Resting too
We must do.
Carol,
Is that you?"

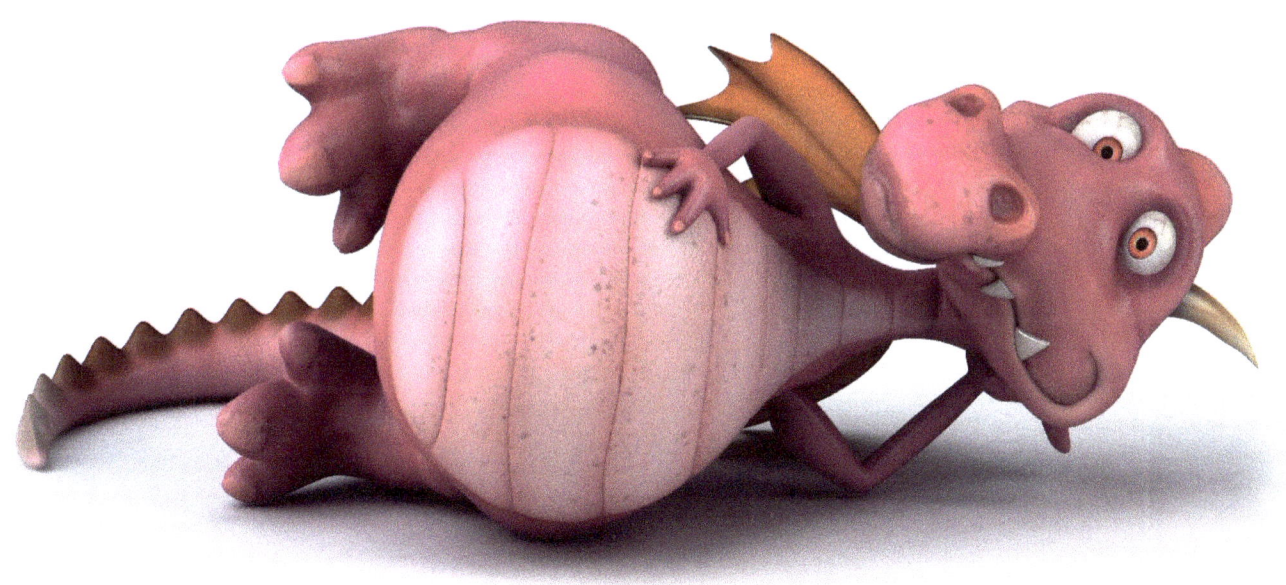

"No, It's Guy,"
 Says Carol.

"He's a shy guy,
 A nice guy.
 A love-to-play guy.
 We like Guy."

Mr. Forgetful Dragon,
Comes to play too.
He rides in a wagon.
Not knowing what to do.

Left shoe on right foot,
Right on left.
He trips over both.
Oh, dear, what next?

THERE ARE MANY OUTDOOR GAMES TO PLAY. PLAY ONE TODAY!

Football, volleyball,
Basketball too,
Dodgeball and soccer.
So much to do.

Baseball,
Frisbee,
Strike a pinata,
Spin till we're dizzy.

Catch,
Skip, bike,
Swim, paddle,
Even hike.

Flip and swing,
Dance and sing,
Run through a sprinkler,
Trampoline!

Hopscotch,
Hula hoop.
Play as one,
Or in a group.

Some call it "fitness,"
Dragons call it "fun."
Join us, won't you?
Everyone!

Please Review This Book

Each review is golden and much appreciated. If you liked this book, could you please leave an honest review? This single act helps the book perform better, supports the author, helps the author improve, and lets other readers know if this book is right for them too! *Thank you!*

Go Here: amazon.com/author/drlindajkeep
Click on your book then scroll down to leave a review.

About the Author

Linda J. Keep, Ph.D. is a parent and grandparent, clinical psychologist, and picture book author. She spent 35 years in private practice and devoted her career to promoting health and wellness. Dr. Keep writes for the enjoyment of children and their families. She writes books that support parents and families in nurturing healthy, happy children who engage in healthy habits.

She is the author of *MR. FORGETFUL DRAGON*, which is her first book in the Dragon Series. This book is also available in French (*M. Dragon Oublieux*) and Spanish (*El Olvidadizo Señor Dragón*). This funny, friendly dragon book promotes kindness and acceptance and features the hilarious antics of this forgetful and sometimes confused dragon. Buy two or three of the set to help with translation skills.

FITNESS IS FUN Outdoor is her second book in the dragon series. Young dragon friends promote wellness in body, mind and spirit through outdoor play. Rediscover games of yesterday and today. See what games the dragons play!

A GIFT FOR YOU!

Visit www.psychologypublications.com/Books to download
12 free maze puzzles & 13 fun coloring pages.

Did you find all the peek-a-boo frogs? (There are 6.)

RESOURCE PAGE

Other children's books on health and fitness that you might enjoy.

1. Oh, The Things You Can Do That Are Good for You: All About Staying Healthy (Cat in the Hat's Learning Library) by Tish Rabe (Author).

2. Breathe Like a Bear: 30 Mindful Moments for Kids to Feel Calm and Focused Anytime, Anywhere by Kira Willey (Author), Anni Betts (Illustrator).

3. Move Your Body!: My Exercise Tips by Gina Bellisario (Author), Renée Kurilla (Illustrator).

4. I am Fearless: A Yoga Story for Kids and Superheroes by Apryl Dawn (Author), Amanda Cottrell (Author).

5. The Busy Body Book: A Kid's Guide to Fitness by Lizzy Rockwell (Author, Illustrator).

6. Anxious Ninja: A Children's Book About Managing Anxiety and Difficult Emotions (Ninja Life Hacks 11) by Mary Nhin (Author), Jelena Stupar (Illustrator).

www.ingramcontent.com/pod-product-compliance
Lightning Source LLC
Chambersburg PA
CBHW061148010526
44118CB00026B/2912